O MAN OF TWO VISIONS! Close one eye and open the other. Close one to the world and all that is therein, and open the other to the hallowed beauty of the Beloved.[1]

Free thyself from the fetters of this world, and loose thy soul from the prison of self ...[2]

Know ye that the embodiment of liberty and its symbol is the animal. That which beseemeth man is submission unto such restraints as will protect him from his own ignorance, and guard him against the harm of the mischief-maker. Liberty causeth man to overstep the bounds of propriety, and to infringe on the dignity of his station. It debaseth him to the level of extreme depravity and wickedness.³

Man possesses two kinds of susceptibilities: the natural emotions, which are like dust upon the mirror, and spiritual susceptibilities, which are merciful and heavenly characteristics. There is a power which purifies the mirror from dust and transforms its reflection into intense brilliancy and radiance so that spiritual susceptibilities may chasten the hearts and heavenly bestowals sanctify them. What is the dust which obscures the mirror? It is attachment to the world, avarice, envy, love of luxury and comfort, haughtiness and self-desire; this is the dust which prevents reflection of the rays of the Sun of Reality in the mirror. The natural emotions are blameworthy and are like rust which deprives the heart of the bounties of God. But sincerity, justice, humility, severance, and love for the believers of God will purify the mirror and make it radiant with reflected rays from the Sun of Truth.[4]

Happiness consisteth of two kinds: physical and spiritual. The physical happiness is limited; its utmost duration is one day, one month, one year. It hath no result. Spiritual happiness is eternal and unfathomable. This kind of happiness appeareth in one's soul with the love of God and suffereth one to attain to the virtues and perfections of the world of humanity. Therefore, endeavour as much as thou art able in order to illumine the lamp of thy heart by the light of love.[5]

Be not the slave of your moods, but their master. But if you are so angry, so depressed and so sore that your spirit cannot find deliverance and peace even in prayer, then quickly go and give some pleasure to someone lowly or sorrowful, or to a guilty or innocent sufferer! Sacrifice yourself, your talent, your time, your rest to another, to one who has to bear a heavier load than you—and your unhappy mood will dissolve into a blessed, contented submission to God.[6]

Supplication to God at morn and eve is conducive to the joy of hearts, and prayer causes spirituality and fragrance. Thou shouldst necessarily continue therein.[7]

O SON OF SPIRIT!
My first counsel is this: Possess a pure, kindly and radiant heart, that thine may be a sovereignty ancient, imperishable and everlasting.[8]

The more we search for ourselves, the less likely we are to find ourselves; and the more we search for God, and to serve our fellow-men, the more profoundly will we become acquainted with ourselves, and the more inwardly assured. This is one of the great spiritual laws of life.[9]

Hear no evil, and see no evil, abase not thyself, neither sigh and weep. Speak no evil, that thou mayest not hear it spoken unto thee, and magnify not the faults of others that thine own faults may not appear great ...[10]

One must see in every human being only that which is worthy of praise. When this is done, one can be a friend to the whole human race. If, however, we look at people from the standpoint of their faults, then being a friend to them is a formidable task.[11]

... If the fire of self overcome you, remember your own faults and not the faults of My creatures, inasmuch as every one of you knoweth his own self better than he knoweth others.[12]

O FRIEND!
In the garden of thy heart plant naught but the rose of love, and from the nightingale of affection and desire loosen not thy hold. Treasure the companionship of the righteous and eschew all fellowship with the ungodly.[13]

To nurse a grievance or hatred against another soul is spiritually poisonous to the soul which nurses it, but to strive to see another person as a child of God and, however heinous his deeds, to attempt to overlook his sins for the sake of God, removes bitterness from the soul and both ennobles and strengthens it.[14]

Set your faces towards unity and let the radiance of its light shine upon you. Gather ye together, and for the sake of God resolve to root out whatever is the source of contention amongst you.[15]

In this sacred Dispensation, conflict and contention are in no wise permitted. Every aggressor deprives himself of God's grace. It is incumbent upon everyone to show the utmost love, rectitude of conduct, straightforwardness and sincere kindliness unto all the peoples and kindreds of the world, be they friends or strangers. So intense must be the spirit of love and loving-kindness, that the stranger may find himself a friend, the enemy a true brother, no difference whatsoever existing between them.[16]

... we should not belittle anyone and call him ignorant, saying: "You know not, but I know." Rather, we should look upon others with respect, and when attempting to explain and demonstrate, we should speak as if we are investigating the truth, saying: 'Here these things are before us. Let us investigate to determine where and in what form the truth can be found.[17]

O CHILDREN OF ADAM!
Holy words and pure and goodly deeds ascend unto the heaven of celestial glory. Strive that your deeds may be cleansed from the dust of self and hypocrisy ... [18]

... defile not your wings with the clay of waywardness and vain desires and suffer them not to be stained with the dust of envy and hate, that ye may not be hindered from soaring in the heavens of My divine knowledge.[19]

Let your eye be chaste, your hand faithful, your tongue truthful and your heart enlightened.[20]

The mind and spirit of man advance when he is tried by suffering. The more the ground is ploughed the better the seed will grow, the better the harvest will be. Just as the plough furrows the earth deeply, purifying it of weeds and thistles, so suffering and tribulation free man from the petty affairs of this worldly life until he arrives at a state of complete detachment. His attitude in this world will be that of divine happiness.[21]

The discerning man rejoiceth at the day of trials, his breast becometh dilated at the time of severe storms, his eyes become brightened when seeing the showers of rain and gusts of wind, whereby trees are uprooted; because he foreseeth the result and the end (of these trials); the leaves, blossoms and fruits (which follow this wintry storm) ...[22]

Meditation is the key for opening the doors of mysteries. In that state man abstracts himself: in that state man withdraws himself from all outside objects; in that subjective mood he is immersed in the ocean of spiritual life and can unfold the secrets of things-in-themselves. To illustrate this, think of man as endowed with two kinds of sight; when the power of insight is being used the outward power of vision does not see.[23]

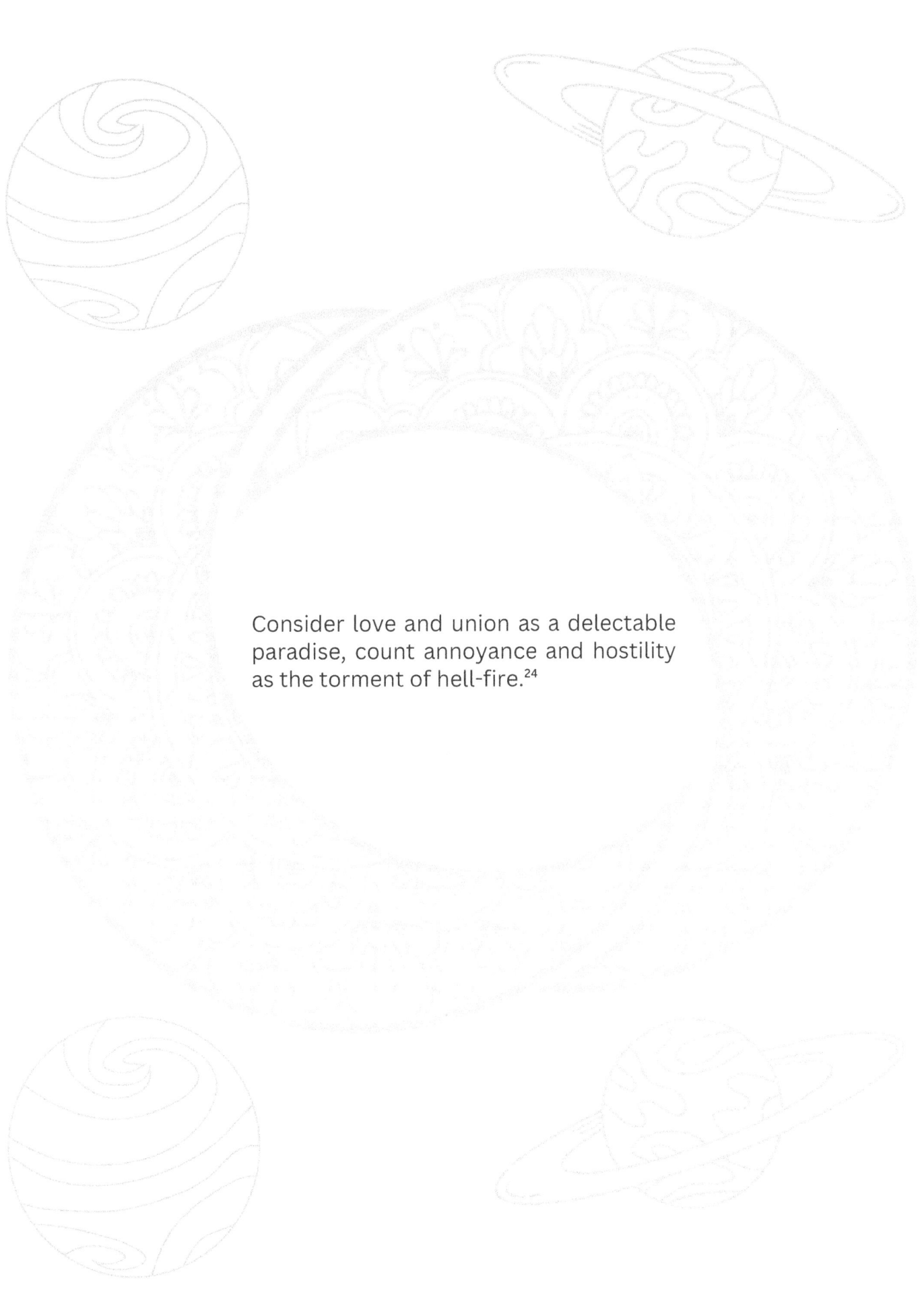

Consider love and union as a delectable paradise, count annoyance and hostility as the torment of hell-fire.[24]

The wrong in the world continues to exist just because people talk only of their ideals, and do not strive to put them into practice. If actions took the place of words, the world's misery would very soon be changed into comfort.[25]

List of References

1. Bahá'u'lláh, The Hidden Words, Part II, from the Persian no. 12
2. The Hidden Words, Part II, from the Persian no. 40
3. Bahá'u'lláh, Gleanings from the Writings of Bahá'u'lláh, No. CLIX
4. 'Abdu'l-Bahá, The Promulgation of Universal Peace, 25 July 1912
5. 'Abdu'l-Bahá, Tablets of Abdul-Baha Abbas, Vol. 3, pp. 673-674
6. Attributed to 'Abdu'l-Bahá in an unpublished English translation of notes in German by Dr. Josephine Fallscheer, taken on 5 August 1910. As the statement is a pilgrim note, it cannot be authenticated.
7. 'Abdu'l-Bahá, Tablets of Abdul-Baha Abbas, p. 186
8. Bahá'u'lláh, The Hidden Words, Part I, from the Arabic, No. 1
9. Shoghi Effendi, Lights of Guidance, No. 391
10. Bahá'u'lláh, The Hidden Words, Part II, from the Persian, No. 44
11. 'Abdu'l-Bahá, Lights of Guidance, No. 319
12. Bahá'u'lláh, The Hidden Words, Part II, from the Persian, No. 66
13. Bahá'u'lláh, The Hidden Words, Part II, from the Persian, No. 3
14. Universal House of Justice to an individual believer, 5 January 1992
15. Bahá'u'lláh, Gleanings from the Writings of Bahá'u'lláh, No. CXI
16. 'Abdu'l-Bahá, Will and Testament of 'Abdu'l-Bahá, Part I, p. 6
17. 'Abdu'l-Bahá, Selections from the Writings of 'Abdu'l-Bahá, No. 15
18. Bahá'u'lláh, The Hidden Words, Part II, from the Persian, No. 69
19. Bahá'u'lláh, The Hidden Words, Part II, from the Persian, No. 26
20. Bahá'u'lláh, Gleanings from the Writings of Bahá'u'lláh, No. CLIII
21. 'Abdu'l-Bahá, Paris Talks, No. 57
22. 'Abdu'l-Bahá, Tablets of Abdul-Baha Abbas, Vol. 1, p. 13
23. 'Abdu'l-Bahá, Paris Talks, No. 54
24. 'Abdu'l-Bahá, Bahá'í World Faith, pp. 355-7
25. 'Abdu'l-Bahá, Paris Talks, No. 1

The authoritative online source of Bahá'í writings is https://www.bahai.org/library